Family Plays

Betty Root

Contents

The Family Joke   2

Sarah's Birthday   9

The Family Joke

> **Cast**
> **Mum**   **Dad**
> **Tim**   **Sarah**
> **Gran**

Tim: Hello, Gran, are you feeling better?

Gran: What?

Sarah: How are you, Gran?

Gran: I'm poorly. My legs hurt and I'm sad.

Sarah: Would you like something to eat?

Gran: No, I'm not hungry. I want cheering up.

Children *(together)*: We'll cheer you up, Gran.

Gran: No you can't. I'm going to bed.

Tim: Goodnight, Gran.

Sarah: Sleep well.

(Exit Gran mumbling.)

(Next evening.)

Sarah: Gran, Gran, what do you think?

Mum *(quietly)***:** Gran's in a mood. Be careful what you say.

Gran: I'm not in a mood.

Tim: I thought you were deaf, Gran.

Mum: She can hear when she wants to.

Sarah: Doesn't anyone want to hear our news?

Dad: What is it Sarah?

Sarah: We're going on the stage.

Mum: Whatever do you mean?

Tim: The school is putting on a play.

Sarah:	And in the interval we have to try to make the audience laugh.
Dad:	See if you can make Gran laugh.
Gran:	I don't feel like laughing. I've got a cold.
Tim:	You ought to see the doctor.
Dad:	I bet you can't make Gran laugh.
Tim:	If we do, will you come and see us at school?
Dad:	I was going to a football match.
Sarah:	Oh please, Dad.

Mum: Of course he will. We all will.

Dad: Only if they make Gran laugh.

Tim: Let's try, Sarah.

(Sarah goes over to Gran.)

Sarah: Who was that lady I saw you with last night?

Tim: That was no lady, that was my Gran.

Gran: I don't think that's very funny.

Tim: How do you make antifreeze?

Sarah: Take away her thermal vest.

Tim: She's beginning to smile.

Gran: No, I'm not.

Sarah: What time is it when the clock strikes thirteen?

Tim: Time to get a new clock.

Mum: Time for a nice cup of tea.

Tim: Oh Mum, Gran was almost laughing then.

Gran: No I wasn't. Anyway I'm going to bed now.

Everyone: Goodnight, Gran.

Sarah: I bet we make you laugh tomorrow.

(Gran, Mum and Dad leave the stage.)

Tim: Shall we dress up tomorrow?

Sarah: And paint our faces.

Tim: What shall we wear?

Sarah: We'll try to look like tramps.

Tim: I'll wear Dad's gardening clothes.

Sarah: I'll wear Mum's old fur coat.

Children *(together):* Isn't it exciting?

(Next evening. Mum, Dad and Gran in the kitchen. Sarah and Tim come in dressed up.)

Tim: Do you think I should play my violin?

Dad: That would make Gran cry, not laugh.

Sarah: I say, I say, what do you give a sea-sick elephant?

Tim: Plenty of room.

Tim: Why did the hedgehog cross the road?

Sarah: To see his flat mate.

Gran: I'm not laughing.

Sarah: Do you know its raining cats and dogs outside?

Tim: Yes I know. I've just stepped in a poodle.

(Mum starts to laugh, then Dad and then Gran.)

Tim: We've made Gran laugh.

Sarah: Just one more joke, Tim.

Tim: Why is Gran like an expensive fish?

Everyone: Because she's a dear old sole.

Gran: Thank you. You have cheered me up. I feel much better now.

Sarah's Birthday

> **Cast**
> **Mum**   **Dad**
> **Sarah**   **Tim**
> **Gran**

(Mum, Dad, Sarah, Tim and Gran sitting round the fire.)

Mum: What do you want for your birthday, Sarah?

Dad: Yes, Sarah, what would you like?

Sarah: I'd like a bird table. Will you make one, Dad?

Mum: Wouldn't you like a new track suit?

Sarah: I don't want clothes, I want a bird table.

Tim: You can put bread for the birds on the lawn. You don't need a bird table.

Sarah: Every day I put bread for the birds on the lawn.

Tim: Well, what's wrong with that?

Sarah: And every day your new dog runs in the garden barking.

Mum: She's right, the dog frightens all the birds away.

Gran: What do you want for your birthday, Sarah?

Sarah: Oh, Gran, please put on your hearing aid.

Gran: How about some new clothes?

(The next day, everyone at breakfast.)

Sarah: Please, Dad, make me a bird table.

Dad: I'll buy you a big box of chocolates.

Sarah: I don't want chocolates. I want a bird table.

Dad: I haven't time. I've got to plant all my seeds in the garden.

Sarah: Please, Dad . . .

Dad: I should have planted the seeds weeks ago.

Mum: Anyone like a cup of tea?

Dad: Not me, I'm too busy.

(Dad rushes out.)

Gran: Time he did something in the garden, it's full of weeds.

Sarah and Tim: We're off to school.

(That evening. Mum, Gran, Sarah and Tim in the kitchen.)

Sarah and Tim: Hello, Mum. Hello, Gran.

Sarah: Where's Dad?

Mum: He's just coming in from the garden.

(Dad enters.)

Dad: Oh dear, I am tired.

Mum: You've been working in the garden all day.

Dad: Yes, and I've planted all my seeds.

Sarah: What are you doing tomorrow, Dad?

Dad: I'm going to work.

Tim: She wants you to make her a bird table.

Dad: I'm too busy, I've lots to do.

Gran: Lazy old thing.

Mum: Now, Gran, that's not true.

Gran: I wish *I* could make her a bird table.

Tim: Why don't you knit one.

Gran: Don't be cheeky.

(Sarah and Tim laugh and go out into the garden.)

Sarah: I know what to do.

Tim: Have you made a plan?

Sarah *(giggling)***:** I'll throw breadcrumbs where Dad has planted his seeds.

Tim: What for?

Sarah: You'll see.

(Next evening, everyone in the kitchen.)

Mum: Tea time, everybody.

Dad: I'm hungry.

Sarah: So are the birds. Look at them on the garden, dad.

Dad: They are all eating my seeds!

(Dad rushes out.)

Mum *(shouts)***:** Don't let your tea get cold.

Gran: What's up with Dad now. Isn't he hungry?

Tim: The birds are eating his seeds.

(Dad comes back.)

Dad: I've frightened them away.

Sarah: Take another look, Dad. They are all back.

(Dad goes to the window and claps his hands.)

Dad: They won't go away. What can I do?

Sarah: I'll make you a scarecrow.

Dad: Thanks, love.

Sarah: *If* you'll make me a bird table.

Dad: I give in, but I'm not very good at making bird tables.

Sarah: And I'm not very good at making scarecrows.

(Next day. Sarah's birthday. Enter Mum, Dad, Gran, Sarah and Tim.)

Everyone: Happy birthday!

Dad: Thanks for putting up the scarecrow, it's frightened the birds away.

Sarah: There are no birds on your seeds now.

Tim *(whispers)***:** Not now they've eaten all the breadcrumbs.

Dad: What's that?

Tim: Nothing, Dad.

(Dad gives Sarah a bird table.)

Sarah: Thanks, Dad.

Tim: I'll put it up for you.

Sarah: Mum, can I have some breadcrumbs?

Mum: Don't take all the bread.

Dad: And put the crumbs on the bird table *(laughs).* Not on my seeds!